Take a Stand!®

Modern American History

Reading, Discussing, and Writing

by John De Gree

**The Classical Historian
San Clemente, California**

DEDICATION

Dedicated to students willing to take a stand

Copyright © 2006 by John De Gree. All rights reserved.
Painting by Fran Johnston, Used with permission, © 2006 by John De Gree. All rights reserved
Edited by Laura Vasquez.
Published by The Classical Historian, San Clemente, California 92673.

No part of this work may be reproduced or transmitted in any form or by any means, electronic or mechanical, including photocopying and recording, or by any information storage or retrieval system without the prior written permission of the publisher. Address inquiries to Take a Stand Publications, 1019 Domador, San Clemente, CA 92673. www.takeastandbooks.com

Table of Contents

Part One: Social Studies Curriculum

Chapter I: Social Studies Essay Questions and Prewriting Activities

1. How the United States Became a World Power — 1
2. Immigration — 5
3. The Role of Religion in American Life — 10
4. U.S. Imperialism — 16
5. Civil Liberties in the 1920s — 20
6. The Great Depression — 25
7. The New Deal — 29
8. World War II in the Pacific — 32
9. The Cold War in the United States — 37
10. The Civil Rights Movement — 42
11. Nixon and Watergate — 46
12. Technology as a Cause for Change — 50
13. Create Your Own Assignment — 54

Part Two: Social Studies Literacy Curriculum

Chapter II: Skills for the One-Paragraph Essay — 55

1. Fact or Opinion? — 55
2. Judgment — 57
3. Supporting Evidence — 58
4. Primary or Secondary Source Analysis — 59
5. Using Quotes — 60
6. Paraphrasing — 61
7. Thesis Statement — 62
8. Conclusion — 63
9. Outline for a One-Paragraph Essay — 64
   Outline Forms for a One-Paragraph Essay — 65
10. Rough Draft of a One-Paragraph Essay — 66
    Rough Draft Forms for a One-Paragraph Essay — 67

Chapter III: Skills for the Five-Paragraph Essay 68
    11.   Taking Notes 68
    12.   Thesis Statement for a Five-Paragraph Essay 69
    13.   The Topic Sentence and the Closer 70
    14.   Outlining a Five-Paragraph Essay 71
           Outline Forms for a Five-Paragraph Essay 72
    15.   Writing a Rough Draft for a Five-Paragraph Essay 74
           Rough Draft Forms for a Five-Paragraph Essay 75
    16.   Revising 77
    17.   Documenting Sources in the Text 78
    18.   Works Cited 79
    19.   Typing Guidelines 80
    20.   The Cover Page and Checklist 80

Chapter IV: Skills for the Multi-Page Essay 81
    21.   Thesis Statement for a Multi-Page Essay 81
    22.   Counterargument 82
    23.   Analyzing Primary Sources 83
    24.   Cause and Effect 84
    25.   Compare and Contrast 85
    26.   Outline and Rough Draft for a Multi-Page Essay 86
           Outline and Rough Draft Forms for a Multi-Page Essay 87

Chapter V: Grading Rubrics 91
    One-Paragraph Essay Grading Rubric 91
    Five-Paragraph Essay Grading Rubric 92
    Multi-Page Essay Grading Rubric 93

Part One: Social Studies Curriculum

Chapter I: Social Studies Essay Questions and Prewriting Activities

1. How the United States Became a World Power
The Effects of the Civil War, Reconstruction, and Urbanization

After U.S. involvement in World War I, there was no doubt that America had entered the world stage as a formidable country. Before World War I, however, the United States was considered a regional power at best. Heeding the words of first President George Washington, Americans hesitated to get involved in world affairs or European wars. The isolationism of eighteenth- and nineteenth-century America changed drastically in the early twentieth century. The United States became an imperialist nation, conquering and controlling many Latin American and Asian lands. The United States was a key reason for the defeat of the Central Powers in World War I. America became an agricultural and industrial powerhouse, setting agricultural and economic examples at which the world could marvel. Various American scientists, inventors, and industrialists set the standard for modernized countries to follow. Furthermore, in World War I, it was the Americans who made the final difference for the Allies.

In your essay, explain the main causes for this drastic change of the United States. Answer the questions: "What caused the United States to change from a regional power to a world power? How was the U.S. different from other countries?" Explore the key factors that enabled the United States to emerge as one of the most powerful countries on earth.

To answer this question well, you should be familiar with these terms and people:

the Civil War	Reconstruction	democracy	capitalism
natural resources	World War I	imperialism	urbanization
Theodore Roosevelt	Woodrow Wilson	European aristocracy	Manifest Destiny
American industrialists and inventors			

This essay has six assignments:

Assignment	Due Date		Due Date
1. Prewriting Activities	_____	4. Rough Draft	_____
2. Thesis Statement	_____	5. Final	_____
3. Outline	_____	6. Works Cited	_____

Copyright © 2006 by John De Gree. All rights reserved

Prewriting Activities
A. Taking Notes

The Civil War

What? _____
Who? _____
When? _____
Where? _____
Why? _____
Did American experiences in the Civil War lead the United States to become a world power? _____
_____

Any other information? _____
_____

Source: _____

Reconstruction

What? _____
Who? _____
When? _____
Where? _____
Why? _____
Did American experiences in Reconstruction lead the United States to become a world power? _____
_____

Any other information? _____
_____

Source: _____

Democracy

What? _____
Who? _____
When? _____
Where? _____
Why? _____
Did the democratic system of government lead the United States to become a world power? _____
_____

Any other information? _____
_____

Source: _____

B. Compare and Contrast:
Nineteenth-Century Europe and Post–Civil War America

By using a variety of sources, compare and contrast the two societies on nineteenth-century Europe and post–Civil War America. Your aim is to try to discover what caused the United States to "catch up" to Europe and even surpass her in terms of agricultural and industrial might. Your goal is to discover "What caused the United States to become a world power in the beginning of the twentieth century?"

1. In the early 1900s, what type of government did most European countries have? _____

2. In Europe, how did people become political leaders? _____

3. In the early 1900s, what type of government did the United States have? _____

4. How did Americans become political leaders? _____

5. Define "aristocracy." In the late nineteenth and early twentieth centuries, did European countries or the United States have an aristocracy? _____

6. What is a serf? _____

7. When were the serfs freed in the Austro-Hungarian Empire? When were serfs freed in Russia? _____

8. When were slaves freed in the United States _____

9. In European countries, who made most decisions involving the economy (e.g., what factories would be built, what farmers would grow)? _____

10. In the United States, who made most decisions involving the economy? _____

11. Compare and contrast the natural resources of European countries with that of the United States. _____

12. What did the United States learn militarily from fighting the Civil War? _____

C. Class Discussion

When you share ideas with other students, your ideas may be reinforced, rejected, or slightly changed. Listening to your classmates' ideas will help you form your own judgment.

Each student must interview at least three classmates who do not sit next to one another. The answers to the following questions must be written down on a piece of paper.

1. What is your name?
2. What led the U.S. to change from being a regional power to a world power?
3. Which facts do you have that support what you think?

Reflection

After you have written down all your classmates' responses, think about them and ask yourself the following questions. Write down your answers under your classmates' responses.

1. What do I think of my classmates' answers?
2. Which are the best answers to question #2 above?
3. Have I changed the way I think?

You should now have a chance to present your ideas in a class discussion. If somebody says something with which you disagree, speak up! In your discussion, you may find out they are actually right, and you are wrong. All possible viewpoints should be valued and defended out loud. Test your ideas in class.

2. Immigration

From 1865 to 1920, nearly 30 million people immigrated to the United States. These immigrants braved a dangerous journey to America for many of the same reasons of those who came before and after them. War, poverty, and lack of financial opportunities pushed people from various nations and continents to the foreign land of America. Once in America, these immigrants faced many difficulties, such as racism, tough living conditions, and the challenges of learning a new language and culture. Even though the challenges were great, people of the world continued to come to the United States by the millions because of the great political, economic, and religious freedoms Americans enjoy.

During this period, some Americans felt that too many immigrants were bad for the country. They questioned the idea that there was enough opportunity in America for all to enjoy. Cities were crowded. Schools were inundated with students who did not know English. Foreigners would work for less pay than native-born Americans. Other Americans welcomed newcomers and thought that immigrants made America strong. Immigrants worked hard and sometimes held two or three jobs. The new industrial America needed unskilled labor, and immigrants provided this. Also, many felt that America was a "nation of nations," as poet Walt Whitman wrote. What made America strong was that it was a melting pot of different cultures and peoples.

In your essay, using 1865–1920 as a historical backdrop, defend or reject the position "Immigration limits are a necessary way to protect the American way of life. Open borders are inherently wrong." Use evidence from 1865 to 1920 to show that you agree or disagree with this quote.

Be familiar with these terms before you write your essay:

industrialization   nativism
political machine   immigration quota
steerage   Homestead Act
Ellis Island   Chinese Exclusion Act of 1882
Webb Alien Land Law   Immigration Restriction Act of 1921
slum

This essay has six assignments:

Assignment	Due Date		Due Date
1. Prewriting Activities	_____	4. Rough Draft	_____
2. Thesis Statement	_____	5. Final	_____
3. Outline	_____	6. Works Cited	_____

Prewriting Activities
A. Taking Notes

Industrialization

What? _____

Who? _____

When? _____

Where? _____

Why? _____

What role did industrialization play in immigration? _____
_____

Any other information? _____
_____

Source: _____

Nativism

What? _____

Who? _____

When? _____

Where? _____

Why? _____

What role did nativism play in immigration? _____
_____

Any other information? _____
_____

Source: _____

Political Machine

What? _____

Who? _____

When? _____

Where? _____

Why? _____

What role did the political machine in immigration? _____
_____

Any other information? _____
_____

Source: _____

B. Immigration to the United States, 1865–1920

Find a graph that shows immigration to the United States during the time period, 1865–1920. If you are able to find a graph showing immigration to the United States at a slightly different time period (for example, 1880–1915), you may use these years as well.

List the number of people who immigrated to the United States from these areas:
1. Northwestern Europe: _____
2. Central Europe: _____
3. Eastern Europe: _____
4. Southern Europe: _____
5. Asia: _____
6. The Americas: _____
7. Africa: _____
8. Oceania: _____

Immigrants and Native-Born Americans from 1865 to 1920

Immigrants to America had different political and economic experiences and religious backgrounds than native-born Americans. Most Americans in 1865 were white Protestants who were accustomed to a democratic society. Some Americans feared that differences with foreigners would negatively change the United States. Choose seven countries from which people emigrated. Research the type of government under which immigrants lived and the kind of religion most practiced in their homeland.

Country of Immigrants	Government	Religion
1. Germany	limited monarch	Lutheran, Roman Catholic
2.		
3.		
4.		
5.		
6.		
7.		

C. Arguments for and against Immigration Limits

List the arguments that were used during the period 1865–1920 for immigration limits and against immigration limits.

Arguments…	
For Immigration Limits	**Against Immigration Limits**
1.	1.
2.	2.
3.	3.
4.	4.
5.	5.

1. Which arguments do you think were the strongest? Why? _____
_____
_____
_____
_____

2. Which arguments do you think are the ones most based on historical fact? _____
_____
_____
_____
_____

3. Which arguments do you think are mostly based on opinions? _____
_____
_____
_____
_____

4. In today's debate on immigration, which of these arguments from the period 1865–1920 are repeated?_____
_____
_____
_____

D. Class Discussion

When you share ideas with other students, your ideas may be reinforced, rejected, or slightly changed. Listening to your classmates' ideas will help you form your own judgment.

Each student must interview at least three classmates who do not sit next to one another. The answers to the following questions must be written down on a piece of paper.

1. What is your name?
2. Defend or reject the position "Immigration limits are a necessary way to protect the American way of life. Open borders are inherently wrong."
3. How did you find your answers?

Reflection

After you have written down all your classmates' responses, think about them and ask yourself the following questions. Write down your answers under your classmates' responses.

1. What do I think of my classmates' answers?
2. Which are the best answers to question #2 above?
3. How have I changed the way I think?

You should now have a chance to present your ideas in a class discussion. If somebody says something with which you disagree, speak up! In your discussion, you may find out they are actually right and you are wrong. All possible viewpoints should be stated and defended out loud. Test your ideas in class.

3. The Role of Religion in American Life

One goal historians have is to study the motives of people. Why did millions decide to immigrate to a land far away, leaving behind family, friends, and familiar places? What were the causes of the great wars in which our nation has been involved? What were determining factors in reformist movements that changed our society? To understand the motive of a culture or of a nation is to grasp better the causes of certain events.

In studying the history of a people, the study of religion is usually a key element to come to understand the motives and aspirations of a nation. The same is true of the American people. In your essay, trace the role religion has played throughout American history. To what extent has religion influenced the politics, economics, and social fabric of the United States? Has religion played a minor role or major one in the life of the American republic?

Be familiar with these terms:

Puritans	Pilgrims	
Salem	the First and Second Great Awakening	
Maryland	Virginia Statute for Religious Freedom	
the First Amendment	the Social Gospel Movement	
Judaism	Catholicism	Protestantism
Christian Fundamentalism	Islamic Fundamentalism	Wall of Separation
Massachusetts Bay Colony		

This essay has six assignments:

Assignment	Due Date		Due Date
1. Prewriting Activities	_____	4. Rough Draft	_____
2. Thesis Statement	_____	5. Final	_____
3. Outline	_____	6. Works Cited	_____

Prewriting Activities
A. Taking Notes

Puritans

What? _____

Who? _____

When? _____

Where? _____

Why? _____

What do the Puritans tell us about religion in America? _____
_____

Any other information? _____
_____

Source: _____

Pilgrims

What? _____

Who? _____

When? _____

Where? _____

Why? _____

What do the Pilgrims tell us about religion in America? _____
_____

Any other information? _____
_____

Source: _____

Massachusetts Bay Colony

What? _____

Who? _____

When? _____

Where? _____

Why? _____

What does the Massachusetts Bay Colony tell us about religion in America? _____
_____

Any other information? _____
_____

Source: _____

B. America's Religions and Institutions

Research the religions practiced in America from the founding of the United States through current times. Based on your research, answer the following questions.

1. About how many religions are represented in the United States of America? _____
   _____

2. What are the top four religions, based on the number of people who profess to belong to that religion? _____
   _____

3. What is the difference between the words "religion" and "faith?" (You can look this up in a dictionary and think about it!) _____
   _____

4. Immigrants to America during these time periods were of what religion?

   1600s: _____

   1700s: _____

   1800–1850: _____

   1850–1900: _____

   1900–1950: _____

5. Were the American Founding Fathers religious men? Did they attend church weekly, pray and write about God and religion? _____
   _____

6. In the American founding papers, such as the Declaration of Independence and the U.S. Constitution, is religion or a belief in God mentioned? How? _____
   _____

8. What does "separation of Church and state" mean? In which document is this phrase first used? Did American Founding Fathers write using the words "separation of Church and state?" _____
   _____
   _____
   _____

C. Class Discussion

When you share ideas with other students, your ideas may be reinforced, rejected, or slightly changed. Listening to your classmates' ideas will help you form your own judgment.

Each student must interview at least three classmates who do not sit next to one another. The answers to the following questions must be written down on a piece of paper.

1. What is your name?
2. Trace the role religion has played throughout American history. To what extent has religion influenced the politics, economics, and social fabric of the U.S.A? Has religion played a minor or a major role in the life of the American republic?
3. What is your supporting evidence?

Reflection

After you have written down all your classmates' responses, think about them and ask yourself the following questions. Write down your answers under your classmates' responses.

1. What do I think of my classmates' answers?
2. Which are the best three answers to question #2 above?
3. Have I changed the way I think?
4. How have I changed the way I think?

You should now have a chance to present your ideas in a class discussion. If somebody says something with which you disagree, speak up! In your discussion, you may find out they are actually right and you are wrong. All possible viewpoints should be stated and defended out loud. Test your ideas in class.

4. U.S. Imperialism

As the young American republic changed from a fledgling democracy to a world power at the middle and end of the nineteenth century, it increasingly faced moral questions regarding the use of its power. Was it morally correct to conquer Mexico and take large sections of Mexican territory in the Mexican Cession? Was it proper to take Cuba, the Philippine Islands, the Hawaiian Islands, and numerous other lands? In the name of the Monroe Doctrine, stability, and at times the spread of democratic and Christian values, the United States intervened tens of times in Latin American and Asian countries. Many questions of the proper use of American power existed in the nineteenth century as they exist today.

In your essay, you will explore various uses of American power in the late nineteenth and early twentieth centuries. In your essay, compare and contrast Theodore Roosevelt's Big Stick diplomacy with Woodrow Wilson's Moral Diplomacy. Which of these foreign policies represents the best use of American power? Why?

You should be familiar with advances and changes in these areas:

Theodore Roosevelt	Woodrow Wilson	Big Stick Diplomacy
Moral Diplomacy	Panama Revolution	Panama Canal
Open Door Policy	Dollar Diplomacy	Imperialism
the Great White Fleet	Howard Taft	World War I
Wilson's 14 Points		

This essay has six assignments:

Assignment	Due Date		Due Date
1. Prewriting Activities	_____	4. Rough Draft	_____
2. Thesis Statement	_____	5. Final	_____
3. Outline	_____	6. Works Cited	_____

Prewriting Activities for Essay #4

A. U.S. Forces Abroad, 1846–1920

1. List the years in which American forces intervened in the following Latin American countries.

   Mexico _____   Guatemala _____

   Honduras _____   Nicaragua _____

   Cuba _____   Haiti _____

   Dominican Republic _____   Puerto Rico _____

   Panama _____

2. List the year in which these Pacific islands were acquired by the United States.

   Philippine Islands _____ Guam _____

   Wake Island _____   Midway Island _____

   Johnston Island _____   Howland Island _____

   Baker Island _____   Hawaiian Islands _____

   Palmyra Island _____   Jarvis Island _____

   American Samoa _____

3. List the year in which American forces were active in the following European countries.

   France _____   Germany _____

   Belgium _____   Luxembourg _____

   Austria-Hungary _____

Copyright © 2006 by John De Gree. All rights reserved

B. Reasons Supporting American Intervention

Briefly describe reasons one might argue supporting American intervention abroad in the years 1846–1920.

C. Reasons Against American Intervention

Briefly describe reasons one might argue against American intervention abroad in the years 1846–1920.

D. Taking Notes

Theodore Roosevelt

What? _____

Who? _____

When? _____

Where? _____

Why? _____

Describe Roosevelt's view of American foreign policy: _____
_____

Any other information? _____
_____

Source: _____

Woodrow Wilson

What? _____

Who? _____

When? _____

Where? _____

Why? _____

Describe Wilson's view of American foreign policy: _____
_____

Any other information? _____
_____

Source: _____

Big Stick Diplomacy

What? _____

Who? _____

When? _____

Where? _____

Why? _____

What is your opinion of this foreign policy: _____
_____

Any other information? _____
_____

Source: _____

E. Class Discussion

When you share ideas with other students, your ideas may be reinforced, rejected, or slightly changed. Listening to your classmates' ideas will help you form your own judgment.

Each student must interview at least three classmates who do not sit next to one another. The answers to the following questions must be written down on a piece of paper.

1. What is your name?
2. Which foreign policy represents the best use of American power — Theodore Roosevelt's Big Stick Diplomacy or Woodrow Wilson's Moral Diplomacy?
3. What is your supporting evidence?

Reflection

After you have written down all your classmates' responses, think about them and ask yourself the following questions. Write down your answers under your classmates' responses.

1. What do I think of my classmates' answers?
2. Which are the best three answers to question #2 above?
3. Have I changed the way I think?
4. How have I changed the way I think?

You should now have a chance to present your ideas in a class discussion. If somebody says something with which you disagree, speak up! In your discussion, you may find out they are actually right and you are wrong. All possible viewpoints should be stated and defended out loud. Test your ideas in class.

5. Civil Liberties in the 1920s

The decade after World War I saw major technological and economic developments. Charles Lindbergh flew an airplane across the Atlantic Ocean in 1927. Throughout the 1920s, Henry Ford's assembly line made it possible for many Americans to own a car. For the first time, Americans bought consumer goods on credit. The standard of living for Americans skyrocketed.

Along with technological and economic developments, the decade called the Roaring Twenties was also one of great social and cultural change. The Nineteenth Amendment gave all American women the right to vote. The role of women in America was changing rapidly. The role of black Americans was also changing. African-Americans contributed greatly to American culture through literature and music in the Harlem Renaissance and the Jazz Age.

As America changed in the 1920s, resistance to this change grew. African-Americans who had immigrated in great numbers to the North faced racial discrimination. Known as the Red Summer, race riots occurred in more than 25 cities during the summer of 1919. Lynching continued throughout the 1920s, and the Ku Klux Klan (KKK) grew to 4 million by 1925. By 1927, however, the KKK diminished greatly in numbers and its power would never be the same.

In your essay, answer the question "Did civil liberties of African-Americans improve, worsen, or stay the same throughout the 1920s?" In your essay, define what civil liberties African-Americans had in 1920. Explore the contributions of African-Americans to American culture in the 1920s. Did these contributions help African-Americans attain more rights?

You should be familiar with these terms and people to answer your question:

Ku Klux Klan of the 1920s	Red Summer	NAACP
civil liberties	the Jazz Age	the Cotton Club
Louis Armstrong	Prohibition	Edward "Duke" Ellington
Dizzy Gillepsie	Harlem Renaissance	Langston Hughes

This essay has six assignments:

Assignment	Due Date		Due Date
1. Prewriting Activities	_____	4. Rough Draft	_____
2. Thesis Statement	_____	5. Final	_____
3. Outline	_____	6. Works Cited	_____

Prewriting Activities

A. Taking Notes

Ku Klux Klan of the 1920s

What? _____

Who? _____

When? _____

Where? _____

Why? _____

What does your research on this term tell you of African-American civil liberties in the 1920s? _____

_____

Source: _____

Red Summer of 1919

What? _____

Who? _____

When? _____

Where? _____

Why? _____

What does your research on this term tell you of African-American civil liberties in the 1920s? _____

_____

Source: _____

NAACP

What? _____

Who? _____

When? _____

Where? _____

Why? _____

What does your research on this term tell you of African-American civil liberties in the 1920s? _____

_____

Source: _____

B. The Jazz Age

Describe in detail artists of the Jazz Age in the following categories:

A. Music: _____

_____

_____

_____

_____

_____

_____

B. Literature: _____

_____

_____

_____

_____

_____

_____

C. Art: _____

_____

_____

_____

_____

_____

_____

Summarize briefly how the Jazz Age changed the United States: _____

_____

_____

_____

_____

_____

_____

_____

_____

C. Civil Liberties in the 1920s

In the 1920s…

1. What was segregation? _____
_____

2. What was lynching and how often did it occur? _____
_____

3. What document freed the slaves in the United States and in what year did this become law? _____
_____

4. After the Civil War, which amendments were written to give civil liberties to African-Americans? What rights did each of these amendments guarantee to all people? _____
_____
_____

5. Did Congress attempt to pass an anti-lynching law in the 1920s? _____
_____

6. There was a mass migration of African-Americans in the United States in the first half of the twentieth century. From where to where did African-Americans migrate? Why did they move? _____
_____
_____

7. How did the NAACP try to fight against discrimination? _____
_____
_____

8. How did the KKK try to take away civil liberties of African-Americans? _____
_____

9. Aside from African-Americans, who else did the KKK hate? _____

10. What civil liberties did many African-Americans not have in the 1920s? _____
_____

E. Class Discussion

When you share ideas with other students, your ideas may be reinforced, rejected, or slightly changed. Listening to your classmates' ideas will help you form your own judgment.

Each student must interview at least three classmates who do not sit next to one another. The answers to the following questions must be written down on a piece of paper.

1. What is your name?
2. Did civil liberties of African-Americans improve, worsen, or stay the same throughout the 1920s?
3. Which facts do you have that support your answer?

Reflection

After you have written down all your classmates' responses, think about them and ask yourself the following questions. Write down your answers under your classmates' responses.

1. What do I think of my classmates' answers?
2. Which are the best three answers to question #2 above?
3. Have I changed the way I think?
4. How have I changed the way I think?

You should now have a chance to present your ideas in a class discussion. If somebody says something with which you disagree, speak up! In your discussion, you may find out they are actually right and you are wrong. All possible viewpoints should be stated and defended out loud. Test your ideas in class.

6. The Great Depression

The Roaring Twenties, a time of incredible growth of the American economy, an era of free-spiritedness that witnessed the flapper and the creation of the Jazz Age, was followed by our nation's worst economic crisis, the Great Depression. From the onset of the Great Depression to the beginning of the Second World War, America struggled for its survival as a free, democratic, and capitalistic society. This struggle for survival cannot be overemphasized; the very fabric of American values was put to the test by the impoverishment of a nation.

In your essay, answer the question "What were the main causes of the Great Depression?"

You should be familiar with these terms.

the Roaring Twenties	Herbert Hoover	Wall Street
overproduction	Dow Jones Industrial Average	Great Crash
the Dust Bowl	The Grapes of Wrath	world depression
speculation	stocks	buying on margin
bankrupt		

This essay has six assignments:

Assignment	Due Date		Due Date
1. Prewriting Activities	_____	4. Rough Draft	_____
2. Thesis Statement	_____	5. Final	_____
3. Outline	_____	6. Works Cited	_____

Prewriting Activities

A. Taking Notes

The Roaring Twenties
What? _____
Who?_____
When?_____
Where?_____
Why?_____
What role did this play in the Great Depression or the New Deal? _____ _____ _____
Source:_____

Herbert Hoover
What? _____
Who?_____
When?_____
Where?_____
Why?_____
What role did this play in the Great Depression or the New Deal?_____ _____ _____
Source:_____

Wall Street
What? _____
Who?_____
When?_____
Where?_____
Why?_____
What role did this play in the Great Depression or the New Deal?_____ _____ _____
Source:_____

B. Causes of the Great Depression

Wall Street   buying on credit   consumer economy   laissez-faire
speculation   buying on margin   overproduction   Great Crash
Dow Jones Industrial Average

Using the above terms and your notes, briefly explain the causes of the Great Depression:

C. Class Discussion

When you share ideas with other students, your ideas may be reinforced, rejected, or slightly changed. Listening to your classmates' ideas will help you form your own judgment.

Each student must interview at least three classmates who do not sit next to one another. The answers to the following questions must be written down on a piece of paper.

1. What is your name?
2. What were the main causes of the Great Depression? How did the U.S. government attempt to battle the problems of this economic crisis? Did the New Deal create a stronger or a weaker America?
3. Where did you find most of your research?

Reflection

After you have written down all your classmates' responses, think about them and ask yourself the following questions. Write down your answers under your classmates' responses.

1. Have I changed my analysis of the causes of the Great Depression based on my classmates' answers? If so, how?
2. Which one of my classmates seems to have the best answers? Where did this person do most of his or her research?

You should now have a chance to present your ideas in a class discussion. If somebody says something with which you disagree, speak up! In your discussion, you may find out they are actually right and you are wrong. All possible viewpoints should be stated and defended out loud. Test your ideas in class.

7. The New Deal

The Great Depression was our country's greatest economic crisis. Factories and mines across America closed. Over 20% of American workers were unemployed. Entire cities of poor people living in cardboard boxes and makeshift wooden homes (named Hoovervilles after President Hoover) formed overnight. Radical political parties, such as the communist and fascist parties, grew in numbers. It looked as if the American system of governance and way of life was in danger.

To combat this economic crisis, Americans elected Franklin Delano Roosevelt. Roosevelt implemented a plan, called the New Deal, to meet America's needs and get the country back on its feet. The New Deal altered the United States, changing the way the federal and state governments interacted as well as altering the relationship between the individual and the state.

In your essay, briefly describe the situation of the United States in the Great Depression and answer the questions "How did Franklin Delano Roosevelt's policies change the United States? Did these changes strengthen America, or weaken it?"

To answer the questions you should be able to address the following terms and people:

the New Deal
Public Works Programs
racial discrimination in the New Deal
New Deal Agencies

Franklin Delano Roosevelt
Social Security
Wheeler-Rayburn Act

This essay has six assignments:

Assignment	Due Date		Due Date
1. Prewriting Activities	_____	4. Rough Draft	_____
2. Thesis Statement	_____	5. Final	_____
3. Outline	_____	6. Works Cited	_____

Prewriting Activities
A. Taking Notes

The New Deal

What? _____

Who? _____

When? _____

Where? _____

Why? _____

How does this person or term relate to the essay topic? _____

_____

_____

Source: _____

Franklin Delano Roosevelt

What? _____

Who? _____

When? _____

Where? _____

Why? _____

How does this person or term relate to the essay topic? _____

_____

_____

Source: _____

Public Works Programs

What? _____

Who? _____

When? _____

Where? _____

Why? _____

How does this person or term relate to the essay topic? _____

_____

_____

Source: _____

B. The New Deal

The New Deal   Franklin Delano Roosevelt   Public Works Programs
New Deal Agencies   Social Security System   discrimination in the New Deal
Federal Communications Commission (FCC)

Using the above terms and your notes, describe the policies of the New Deal:

C. Class Discussion

When you share ideas with other students, your ideas may be reinforced, rejected, or slightly changed. Listening to your classmates' ideas will help you form your own judgment.

Each student must interview at least three classmates who do not sit next to one another. The answers to the following questions must be written down on a piece of paper.

1. What is your name?
2. How did Franklin Delano Roosevelt's policies change the United States? Did these changes strengthen America, or weaken it?
3. Where did you find most of your research?

Reflection

After you have written down all your classmates' responses, think about them and ask yourself the following questions. Write down your answers under your classmates' responses.

1. Have I changed my analysis of the causes of World War I based on my classmates' answers? If so, how?
2. Which one of my classmates seems to have the best answers? Where did this person do most of his or her research?

You should now have a chance to present your ideas in a class discussion. If somebody says something with which you disagree, speak up! In your discussion, you may find out they are actually right and you are wrong. All possible viewpoints should be stated and defended out loud. Test your ideas in class.

8. World War II in the Pacific

World War I was a war of incredible and catastrophic scope. During this conflict, some called it the War to End All Wars. However, this war may have caused the Russian Revolution, the rise of Hitler, World War II, and the disillusionment of a generation. For the next 70 years, the effects of World War I could be felt throughout the world. World War II (1939–1945) caused the death of over 30 million people and may have led to the enslavement of tens of millions in totalitarian regimes.

To end the war in the Pacific, the United States decided to drop atomic bombs on the Japanese cities of Hiroshima and Nagasaki. In dropping these bombs, President Truman decided that he would save more lives by using the awesome power of this new technology rather than invading and conquering Japan. After the war, some have argued that dropping these bombs on civilian populations was wrong.

In your essay, answer the question "Was the United States morally correct to drop the atomic bomb on Hiroshima and Nagasaki?" In your answer, discuss the nature of the battles against the Japanese in the Pacific, and research what a full-scale invasion of Japan would have cost both Japanese and Americans.

To answer this question, you should be familiar with these terms and people as they relate to World War II in the Pacific:

Bataan Death March	Midway	Iwo Jima
Guadalcanal	Battle of Philippines	Prisoners of War
Douglas MacArthur	Albert Einstein	Manhattan Project
Harry S. Truman	Okinawa	

This essay has six assignments:

Assignment	Due Date		Due Date
1. Prewriting Activities	_____	4. Rough Draft	_____
2. Thesis Statement	_____	5. Final	_____
3. Outline	_____	6. Works Cited	_____

Prewriting Activities
A. Taking Notes

Bataan Death March

What? _____
Who? _____
When? _____
Where? _____
Why? _____
What does this say about the nature of the war in the Pacific? _____
_____
_____
Source: _____

Midway

What? _____
Who? _____
When? _____
Where? _____
Why? _____
What does this say about the nature of the war in the Pacific? _____
_____
_____
Source: _____

Iwo Jima

What? _____
Who? _____
When? _____
Where? _____
Why? _____
What does this say about the nature of the war in the Pacific? _____
_____
_____
Source: _____

B. The Fighting in the Pacific

Based on your research of the terms and people, answer these questions:

1. Describe the fighting in the Pacific.
a) How did the Japanese soldier fight? (e.g., fiercely, weakly) _____

b) How did he view the idea of surrendering? _____

c) How did the Japanese treat American soldiers who surrendered? _____

d) What does the Japanese practice of the "kamikazi" tell you about the Japanese soldier? _____

2. What role did General Douglas MacArthur have in the war in the Pacific? _____

3. Which scientist urged President Franklin Delano Roosevelt to begin work on an atomic bomb? _____

4. From where had this scientist emigrated? Why did he leave his home country and become an American? _____

5. Why did this scientist want Roosevelt to create this bomb as quickly as possible? _____

6. What was the name of the secret project the U.S. government funded to create the atomic bomb? _____

7. To compare American bombing of Japan with bombing in Europe, name cities that were destroyed by aerial bombing in Germany during World War II? How many civilians were killed in these bombings? _____

C. Class Discussion

When you share ideas with other students, your ideas may be reinforced, rejected, or slightly changed. Listening to your classmates' ideas will help you form your own judgment.

Each student must interview at least three classmates who do not sit next to one another. The answers to the following questions must be written down on a piece of paper.

1. What is your name?
2. Was the United States morally correct to drop the atomic bomb on Hiroshima and Nagasaki?
3. How did you find your answers?

Reflection

After you have written down all your classmates' responses, think about them and ask yourself the following questions. Write down your answers under your classmates' responses.

1. What do I think of my classmates' answers?
2. Which are the best answers to question #2 above?
2. Why do I think this?

You should now have a chance to present your ideas in a class discussion. If somebody says something with which you disagree, speak up! In your discussion, you may find out they are actually right and you are wrong. All possible viewpoints should be stated and defended out loud. Test your ideas in class.

9. The Cold War in the United States

In World War II, the U.S. had two main goals: stop Japan and Germany from expanding. In these two aspects Americans achieved success. The Allies destroyed the militaristic regimes of Japan and Germany and erected new democratic societies in both of these lands. However, the peace of World War II did not bring U.S. troops home. U.S. troops did not come home after World War II, and they still are stationed in western Europe.

After World War II, the world was split into two main camps, the communist nations and the democratic nations. American soldiers stationed in Europe and Asia stayed and fought to counter communism and the Soviet Union. Latin America also became the battleground of ideas of communism and democracy. A new kind of war began for America and the world, the Cold War.

In your essay, trace the development of the Cold War from its beginnings through the 1960s, focusing mainly on the effects of the Cold War in the United States. Answer the question "How did the Cold War affect American society, 1945–1969?" To answer this question fully, you need to understand the nature of the Cold War, the Soviet government of communism, and the U.S. support of democracy.

You should be familiar with these terms and people as they apply to the Cold War:

communism	totalitarianism	democracy
Vladimir Lenin	Josef Stalin	human rights
the Potsdam Conference	the Soviet Bloc	the Iron Curtain
containment	the Loyalty Program	McCarran-Walter Act
Ethel and Julius Rosenberg	Joseph McCarthy	domino theory
House Un-American Activities Committee (HUAC)		

This essay has six assignments:

Assignment	Due Date		Due Date
1. Prewriting Activities	_____	4. Rough Draft	_____
2. Thesis Statement	_____	5. Final	_____
3. Outline	_____	6. Works Cited	_____

Prewriting Activities
A. Taking Notes

Follow the structure below to write notes.

Communism

What?_____

Who?_____

When?_____

Where?_____

Why?_____

Any other information? _____

_____

Source:_____

Totalitarianism

What?_____

Who?_____

When?_____

Where?_____

Why?_____

Any other information? _____

_____

Source:_____

Democracy

What?_____

Who?_____

When?_____

Where?_____

Why?_____

Any other information? _____

_____

Source:_____

B. The Rise of Communism

1. What are the main points of *The Communist Manifesto* (1848) by Karl Marx and Robert Engels? _____
_____
_____

2. What kind of government did Russia have in 1916? _____

3. What were the problems in Russia in 1916? _____

4. Who were the Bolsheviks and when did they take over Russia? _____
_____

5. In 1920, who were the top three Bolsheviks in Russia? _____

6. Under Vladimir Lenin, Russia reorganized into a federation. What was the new name of the country? _____
_____

7. In the Soviet Union what freedoms were denied? What could people not do, nor say, that Americans could? _____
_____

8. What did the Communists do to private property and to Church property? Why? ____
_____

9. After Lenin died who took over in the Soviet Union? _____

10. What was the Five-Year Plan? _____

11. How many civilian lives were killed because of communism? _____
_____

12. The Soviet Union is known as the world's first modern totalitarian state. Why was it called totalitarian? _____
_____

13. How long did the Communists remain in power in the Soviet Union? _____

14. In a Communist state, who or what is more important, the state or the individual? ___
_____

15. Does communism continue the tradition of western political thought, begun by the Greco-Roman and Judeo-Christian cultures? How or how not? _____
_____

C. U.S. Policy against Communism, 1945–1969

1. Who was at the Potsdam Conference at the end of World War II? What was decided among these leaders? _____
_____
_____

2. What happened in the countries occupied by the Soviet Union after World War II? ___
_____
_____

3. What was the Berlin Airlift? Why did the United States help the West Berliners? ___
_____
_____

4. What was the Marshall Plan? Who participated in the Marshall Plan? _____
_____
_____

5. What was the effect of the Marshall Plan on the countries that participated? _____
_____
_____

6. Why did most Americans not trust the Communists in the Soviet Union? _____
_____
_____

7. In the United States, what law or laws showed that Americans were afraid of communism within America? _____
_____

8. What did the House Un-American Activities Committee (HUAC) investigate? _____
_____

9. Who were the Hollywood Ten? _____
_____

10. Briefly research the Kennedy-Nixon election of 1960. How did the U.S. policy against communism affect this election? _____
_____
_____

11. How did some Americans prepare for a third world war against the Soviet Union? (What did they build in their backyard?) _____

D. Class Discussion

When you share ideas with other students, your ideas may be reinforced, rejected, or slightly changed. Listening to your classmates' ideas will help you form your own judgment.

Each student must interview at least three classmates who do not sit next to one another. The answers to the following questions must be written down on a piece of paper.

1. What is your name?
2. How did the Cold War affect American society, 1945–1969?
3. How did you find your answers?

Reflection

After you have written down all your classmates' responses, think about them and ask yourself the following questions. Write down your answers under your classmates' responses.

1. What do I think of my classmates' answers?
2. Which answer is the best to question #2 above?

You should now have a chance to present your ideas in a class discussion. If somebody says something with which you disagree, speak up! In your discussion, you may find out they are actually right and you are wrong. All possible viewpoints should be stated and defended out loud. Test your ideas in class.

10. The Civil Rights Movement

Although Thomas Jefferson's original draft of the Declaration of Independence included the abolition of slavery in America, delegates to the Second Continental Congress would not approve. Jefferson had to strike the end of slavery from the document. Since the beginning of the United States of America, Americans lived in a country built on contradicting ideas. How could a nation formed on the idea that "all men are created equal" enslave other humans?

In 1865, the U.S. government ended the ancient practice of slavery with the passage of the thirteenth amendment. With the fourteenth and fifteenth amendments, many Americans hoped that all Americans would enjoy the freedoms that form the ideals of the American way of life. Unfortunately, for most African-Americans, life in America was a bitter promise unfulfilled. After the Civil War, segregation was the norm in most states, and blacks lived as inferior citizens. Denied the right to vote, unprotected by police, unable to attend high-quality schools, black Americans were subjected to a life of oppression and violence. Some white Americans terrorized, beat, raped, and killed black Americans. Although black Americans sacrificed themselves in America's wars, paid taxes, and contributed in every way to American life, they were forced to live as second-class citizens.

In the 1940s, 1950s and 1960s, Americans worked to change the unjust policy of racial segregation. Leaders of this civil rights movement worked towards equal protection of the laws for all Americans, regardless of race. These leaders risked their lives to bring constitutional rights to all. In your essay, research the biographies of these Americans: A. Philip Randolph, Martin Luther King, Jr., Malcolm X, Thurgood Marshall, James Farmer, and Rosa Parks. Answer the question "Which of these leaders did the most to promote civil rights in the United States?"

You should be familiar with these terms and people:
A. Philip Randolph   Martin Luther King, Jr.   Malcolm X
Thurgood Marshall   Rosa Parks   *Brown v. Board of Education*
Jackie Robinson   James Farmer   Montgomery bus boycott
Little Rock, Arkansas   the Civil Rights Act of 1964
Black Panther Movement   Elijah Muhammad
National Association for the Advancement of Colored People (NAACP)

This essay has six assignments:

Assignment	Due Date		Due Date
1. Prewriting Activities	_____	4. Rough Draft	_____
2. Thesis Statement	_____	5. Final	_____
3. Outline	_____	6. Works Cited	_____

Prewriting Activities
A. Taking Notes

Follow the structure below to write notes.

A. Philip Randolph

What?_____
Who?_____
When?_____
Where?_____
Why?_____
How important was this person to the civil rights movement? _____
_____
_____

Source:_____

Martin Luther King, Jr.

What?_____
Who?_____
When?_____
Where?_____
Why?_____
How important was this person to the civil rights movement?_____
_____
_____

Source:_____

Malcolm X

What?_____
Who?_____
When?_____
Where?_____
Why?_____
How important was this person to the civil rights movement?_____
_____
_____

Source:_____

B. The Civil Rights Movement

1. Describe racial segregation in the United States before 1950. _____

2. What Supreme Court decision approved of racial segregation? _____

3. Do you think that this Supreme Court decision (in answer #3) was just or unjust? Explain your answer. _____

4. Name one thing Truman did to promote civil rights of all Americans. _____

5. What was the *Brown v. Board of Education* case? _____

6. What role did the philosophy of nonviolence play in the civil rights movement? _____

7. Describe the Montgomery bus boycott. _____

8. What was the Southern California Leadership Conference? _____

9. What was the Student Nonviolent Coordinating Committee? _____

10. Describe a sit-in. _____

11. Describe freedom rides. _____

12. What was the Albany movement? _____

13. What was the march on Washington? _____

14. Summarize Dr. King's speech at the March on Washington. _____

15. What were the Civil Rights Act of 1964 and the Voting Rights Act of 1965? _____

16. What is the Nation of Islam? _____

17. Describe the Black Power Movement. _____

C. Class Discussion

When you share ideas with other students, your ideas may be reinforced, rejected, or slightly changed. Listening to your classmates' ideas will help you form your own judgment.

Each student must interview at least three classmates who do not sit next to one another. The answers to the following questions must be written down on a piece of paper.

1. What is your name?
2. Which leader did the most to promote civil rights in the United States?
3. Why did you choose this leader over the others?

Reflection

After you have written down all your classmates' responses, think about them and ask yourself the following questions. Write down your answers under your classmates' responses.

1. What do I think of my classmates' answers?
2. Which answers were the best to questions #2 and #3?

You should now have a chance to present your ideas in a class discussion. If somebody says something with which you disagree, speak up! In your discussion, you may find out they are actually right and you are wrong. All possible viewpoints should be stated and defended out loud. Test your ideas in class.

11. Nixon and Watergate

The 1960s are known as a time of great social change in the United States. The successes of the civil rights movement brought many African-Americans into the American political process. Ethnic minorities demanded equal treatment. The traditional role of women in American society was challenged. The Nixon years, 1968–1974, began as what seemed a reestablishment of traditional American ways. Richard Nixon spoke against the counterculture in America, claiming to support the silent majority. He spoke ardently of the need for law and order to combat the war protests that were at times violent.

Even though Nixon seemed to represent the establishment of law and order, it was during his presidency that one of the greatest presidential scandals in U.S. history occurred. This scandal was tied to President Nixon and forced him from office. The Watergate scandal is perhaps the greatest known scandal of a U.S. president. Not only did Nixon's activities regarding this scandal force him to resign, but this scandal has also affected U.S. politics in a variety of ways ever since.

In your essay, describe the events and main politicians of the Watergate scandal. Answer the question "What was the Watergate scandal and what was its greatest effect on America?"

You should be familiar with these terms and people:

Enemies List	the plumbers	Vietnam (1975)
Cambodia (1975)	Committee to Reelect the President	Washington Post
Woodward and Bernstein	checks and balances	Ford Administration
War Powers' Act	G. Gordon Liddy	

This essay has six assignments:

Assignment	Due Date		Due Date
1. Prewriting Activities	_____	4. Rough Draft	_____
2. Thesis Statement	_____	5. Final	_____
3. Outline	_____	6. Works Cited	_____

Prewriting Activities
A. Taking Notes

Follow the structure below to write notes.

Enemies List
What?_____
Who?_____
When?_____
Where?_____
Why?_____
How was this term or person important to the Watergate scandal? _____
_____
Source:_____

---

the Plumbers
What?_____
Who?_____
When?_____
Where?_____
Why?_____
How was this term or person important to the Watergate scandal? _____
_____
Source:_____

G. Gordon Liddy
What?_____
Who?_____
When?_____
Where?_____
Why?_____
How was this term or person important to the Watergate scandal? _____
_____
Source:_____

B. The Watergate Scandal

1. What was the Committee to Reelect the President, under President Nixon? _____

2. Name key members on this Committee _____

3. What were some illegal activities in which the Committee to Reelect the President was involved? _____

4. What did the Plumbers want to break into at the Watergate Hotel? _____

5. Did President Nixon order the break-in at the Watergate Hotel? _____

6. What did Nixon do involving the Watergate break-in that was illegal? _____

7. What does "obstruction of justice" mean? _____

8. How did the American public learn of the illegal activities at the Watergate Hotel? _____

9. What is a "special prosecutor?" _____

10. Was Nixon impeached? How did he leave office? _____

11. How did the Watergate scandal influence the Ford presidency? _____

12. After President Nixon resigned, North Vietnamese Communists conquered South Vietnam. Was this a result of Nixon resigning? Why or why not? _____

13. Did Americans change the way they view their government after the Watergate scandal? Is so or if not, what proof do you have of this? _____

C. Class Discussion

When you share ideas with other students, your ideas may be reinforced, rejected, or slightly changed. Listening to your classmates' ideas will help you form your own judgment.

Each student must interview at least three classmates who do not sit next to one another. The answers to the following questions must be written down on a piece of paper.

1. What is your name?
2. What was the Watergate scandal and how did it affect America?

Reflection

After you have written down all your classmates' responses, think about them and ask yourself the following questions. Write down your answers under your classmates' responses.

1. What do I think of my classmates' answers?
2. Which answer is the best to question #2 above?

You should now have a chance to present your ideas in a class discussion. If somebody says something with which you disagree, speak up! In your discussion, you may find out they are actually right and you are wrong. All possible viewpoints should be stated and defended out loud. Test your ideas in class.

12. Technology as a Cause for Change

In the study of history, it is important to study people, places, and events. However, the role of technology must not be overlooked. Technology has played an incredibly important role in history. Think what life was like before the invention of the wheel. Roman aqueducts made it possible for large cities to exist far from sources of water. The Hittites mastered the creation of bronze and dominated their neighbors. The underground sewage system saved civilizations from terrifying diseases. The Gutenberg press made it possible for modern ideas to spread rapidly in Europe. Imagine what it must have been like for soldiers to fight against tanks for the first time on a battlefield.

When a great change occurs in civilization, it is referred to as a "revolution." In this sense, society alters greatly from what was before. In the Industrial Revolution, the workplace changed from the farm to the factory. Men, women, and children left the confines of the home and farm to work in occupations that did not exist before. With greater freedoms in the workplace, social changes occurred. The right to vote spread to women. Cities grew. Because of larger cities, service professions flourished. In the industrial revolution, man created better and faster forms of transportation.

Recently, many historians have written that humankind is in another type of revolution, the Technological Revolution. The incredible number of inventions in the past 50 to 60 years has radically altered life. In your essay, research changes in information of the past half century and answer the question "In what facet of life have technological advances in the Information Age changed the United States?"

Research these terms and people:

computer	Steve Jobs	Apple	IBM	e-mail	mobile phone
hardware	software	Internet	service jobs	facsimile	WWW
Bill Gates	CD-ROM	globalization	Electronic	computer network	
telecommunications					

This essay has six assignments:

Assignment	Due Date		Due Date
1. Prewriting Activities	_____	4. Rough Draft	_____
2. Thesis Statement	_____	5. Final	_____
3. Outline	_____	6. Works Cited	_____

Prewriting Activities
A. Taking Notes

Follow the structure below to write notes.

Computer

What?_____

Who?_____

When?_____

Where?_____

Why?_____

How is this person or term important to the information age? _____

_____

Source:_____

Steve Jobs

What?_____

Who?_____

When?_____

Where?_____

How is this person or term important to the information age? _____

_____

Source:_____

Apple

What?_____

Who?_____

When?_____

Where?_____

How is this person or term important to the information age? _____

_____

Source:_____

When taking these notes, think how technology of the Information Age has changed the U.S.

Copyright © 2006 by John De Gree. All rights reserved

B. The Technological Revolution

1. Write a summary of how you personally use technology of the information age in your daily life. _____

2. Write how communication technology played a role in the everyday life of somebody your age before 1940. _____

3. Choose a large employer in the United States. (for example, the U.S. military, an airplane company, a school district, a theme park). Write how reality has changed for this employer in the last 50 to 60 years. _____

4. In what area of American life has technology of the information age changed the United States the most? _____

C. Class Discussion

When you share ideas with other students, your ideas may be reinforced, rejected, or slightly changed. Listening to your classmates' ideas will help you form your own judgment.

Each student must interview at least three classmates who do not sit next to one another. The answers to the following questions must be written down on a piece of paper.

1. What is your name?
2. In what facet of life have technological advances in the information age changed the United States?
3. Why do you think this?

Reflection

After you have written down all your classmates' responses, think about them and ask yourself the following questions. Write down your answers under your classmates' responses.

1. What do I think of my classmates' answers?
2. With which student do I most agree and why?
3. With which student do I most disagree and why?

You should now have a chance to present your ideas in a class discussion. If somebody says something with which you disagree, speak up! In your discussion, you may find out they are actually right and you are wrong. All possible viewpoints should be stated and defended out loud. Test your ideas in class.

13. Create Your Own Assignment

Now that you have had much experience in researching a topic, taking a stand and defending it, and writing a top-quality persuasive essay, create your own assignment! Here are some ideas:

Immigration to the United States, 1950–2000: Open, Limited, or Closed Borders?

The War in Iraq: Right, or Wrong?

Separation of Powers in the Twentieth and Twenty-first Centuries:

> Does the President Have Too Much Power?
> Does Congress Have Too Much Power?
> Does the Supreme Court Have Too Much Power?

Why Has There Been an Increase in Out of Wedlock Births?

What are the Effects of the Great Society?

Has the U.S. National Park System Respected Both the Environment and Property Rights?

Carter and Reagan Presidencies: Compare and Contrast

Changing Rights of Women 1800–2000. How Has Life Changed?

How Has U.S. Foreign Policy Affected the Middle East, 1900–Present?

Compare and Contrast Religious Liberty in the United States, 1800 with 2005

Trace the Emergence of the Labor Movement in the United States

The United States: City on a Hill?

Twentieth-Century America: An Extension of the Founding, or a Different Country?

American Pop Culture: Good — or Bad — for Americans?

Part Two: Social Studies Literacy Curriculum

Chapter II: Skills for the One-Paragraph Essay

1. Fact or Opinion?

A **fact** in history is a statement that is accepted as true and is not debatable. A fact often refers to a date, a person, or a document. For example, "The Declaration of Independence was written and signed in 1776." We know this happened because we have the original document, the men who wrote and signed this document wrote about it, and observers wrote about it as well. There is no doubt in anybody's mind whether the facts in this statement are true.

Which of these sentences are facts?

Fact or Not a Fact?
1. _____ The American Civil War was fought 1860–1865.
2. _____ General Grant led the Union forces to victory.
3. _____ President Woodrow Wilson loved fighting wars.
4. _____ Ronald Reagan was U.S. president from 1976–1982.
5. _____ Global warming caused the hottest day in the year 2004.

Opinion

An **opinion** is an expression of somebody's ideas and is debatable. Opinions that are based on facts and good reasoning are stronger than opinions not based on facts. In history, opinions alone tend to be less persuasive than when a person supports his opinions with facts.

Which of the following are opinions and which are facts?

Opinion or Fact?
1. _____ Western political thought is harmful to people.
2. _____ German aggression caused World War I.
3. _____ History is the best school subject because of the awesome teachers.
4. _____ The Japanese bombed Pearl Harbor.
5. _____ The United States caused the Cold War.

Copyright © 2006 by John De Gree. All rights reserved

Now that you've learned the difference between fact and opinion, read the example paragraphs below and answer the questions.

Student 1: The United States of America has always been a country that has favored imperialism. Many Americans feel that they have the right to expand their way of government, and their religion, to other places. Americans think that because they are strong, they must be right. One American put it this way, "If we know the right way to do something, aren't we obligated to let the world know?" If you look at the U.S. history from 1800 to 2000, there are many instances of American intervention abroad. Study Latin America. Look at the history of Mexico. There are horrible examples here of Yankee imperialism.

Student 2: At times, the United States of America has favored expansion and imperialism. In the 1800s, the United States conquered North America by pushing the Indians onto reservations, by defeating Mexico in the Mexican-American War (1846–48), and by defeating Spain in the Spanish-American War (1898). In the Mexican-American War, the United States took the Mexican Cession from Mexico, an area almost half the size of Mexico. In the Spanish-American War, the United States took the Caribbean island of Cuba, along with islands in the Pacific Ocean — such as the Philippines and Guam. However, at other times, the United States has chosen not to conquer land and people — such as in Europe after World War II.

Questions
1. Which of these two students uses more opinion than fact? _____

2. Copy one sentence that is an opinion. _____

3. Copy one sentence that details at least one fact. _____

4. Which of these two students' writings uses more historical evidence to back up the topic sentence? Does this historical evidence make the paragraph more persuasive, or less? Why? _____

2. Judgment

Judgment in social studies means a person's evaluation of facts. For example, the French Revolution began in 1789. This year was very important for France. The fact in these sentences is that the French Revolution began in 1789. The judgment is that this year was important for France. Good judgment is very persuasive but bad judgment is not. With your teacher make one judgment per fact below. Discuss your judgments in class.

Fact:	More Americans lost their lives in the American Civil War than in any other war.
Judgment:	The Civil War was extremely difficult for many American families.
Fact:	Franklin Delano Roosevelt was elected a record four times as U.S. President.
Judgment:	Americans greatly trusted Roosevelt to be the leader of the country.

Make your own.

Fact:	
Judgment:	
Fact:	
Judgment:	
Fact:	
Judgment:	

3. Supporting Evidence

Supporting evidence refers to everything you use to support your thesis. These include but are not limited to the following.

1. Diaries and journals
2. Government documents, such as birth certificates
3. Songs and stories
4. Coins, medals, jewelry
5. Artistic works such as pictures and paintings
6. Tools and pottery
7. Documents, such as the Declaration of Independence
8. Weapons
9. Burial remains
10. Literature and customs

Good writers can overwhelm the reader with so many pieces of supporting evidence that the writing will be quickly accepted. Also, the writer has a duty to explain carefully and logically the meaning of the evidence, showing how it supports the thesis. A writer must be careful, however, not to include unnecessary evidence. For example, the fact that Lincoln was born in a log cabin isn't evidence that he was a good president. Also, the dates a president was born and died may be evidence, but they would not support a thesis arguing who was the best president.

Practice
With your teacher discuss which of the following is evidence for the topic "Explain what daily life was like in the United States of America in the 1900s.
1. A diary from 1984
2. A newspaper article from 1799
3. Your friend likes the subject
4. A documentary about American life in the Twentieth century
5. An American song written and sung in 1968
6. Information on America's leaders of the 1900s
7. A painting of farm life in 1600s America

4. Primary or Secondary Source Analysis

A **primary source** is a piece of evidence authored by a person who witnessed or experienced a historical event. For example, diaries and journals are primary sources. It is usually better to find out something from a person who experienced a particular event than to hear about it secondhand. Primary source documents are usually the most useful for historians.

A **secondary source** is a piece of evidence developed by somebody who was not a witness to the historical event. Examples of secondary sources are textbooks, documentaries, and encyclopedias. Secondary sources are valuable but not as valuable as primary sources. Secondary sources contain the bias of the writer. This means that the writer of a secondary source will put his own ideas into his explanation of the historical event, even when he may be trying not to.

   Take a look at these two examples regarding the same event
   Event: a car accident outside of school

Example 1: "Oh no! I was in the back seat of my mom's car. This kid threw his friend's handball onto the street. All of a sudden, his friend jumped in front of my mom's car to get his ball. He didn't even look if a car was coming. My mom hit him and his body smashed against our windshield. Blood was everywhere!"

Example 2: "Did you hear what happened? Mario told me that his brother was walking home when he dropped his handball onto the street. After his brother looked both ways for cars, he stepped out onto the street to get his ball. Then this mad lady came speeding down the street and aimed her car at him. She hit him on purpose!"

Questions
1. Which is a primary source? _____
2. Which is a secondary source? _____
3. Which of these is more believable? Why? _____

5. Using Quotes

An effective analytical essay in social studies will use quotes. For example, an essay about the Declaration of Independence will be stronger if certain passages from this document are used. When you argue a point about the past, there is no better evidence than a quote from a primary source. Also, when you use quotes, it is essential that you frame the quote. Before the quote is used, you need to introduce it. Introducing a quote means to write the original author's name and the speech or document from which the quote was taken, and to explain the quote briefly. Then write the quote. After you write the quote, tell the reader its meaning. It is your job to lead the reader through the quote, so your main point is emphasized. Do not imagine the reader will understand exactly what you mean, unless you tell the reader exactly what you are thinking.

Look at the example below. The paragraph is part of an answer to the question "According to Thomas Jefferson, is there anybody in society who should have more rights than others?"

According to Thomas Jefferson, all men should have the same rights in society. In the Declaration of Independence, Jefferson writes, "All men are created equal; that they are endowed by their Creator with certain unalienable rights; that among these are life, liberty, and the pursuit of happiness." This means that each person should be treated equally under the law. Whether you are rich or poor, or whether your family is famous or not, all citizens should have the same rights.

Practice
Practice framing three quotations taken from your textbook. Use correct punctuation.

1. _____

2. _____

3. _____

6. Paraphrasing

Paraphrasing means to take information from your research and to put it in your own words. This is an important skill to have when writing a research paper. If you copy directly from a source such as a book, but do not place the words in quotation marks and write the author's name, it is called **plagiarism**. Plagiarism is against the rules of writing and your teacher will not accept the work! The law may punish a professor or an author for plagiarizing.

Here is an example of paraphrasing a quote from a teacher.

Quote:
"In 1914, European nations began a war that was caused by dislike and hatred among countries. The United States tried to stay out of the war by being neutral. After German sailors aboard a submarine killed Americans on the British ship the *Lusitania*, President Woodrow Wilson grew to believe that Germany was a danger, and persuaded the U.S. Congress to declare war in 1917."

Paraphrase:
European nations began fighting World War I because of old rivalries. Woodrow Wilson's attempt to keep the United States out of the war succeeded for some time. Nevertheless, German actions affected American citizens. A German submarine destroyed the British ship, the *Lusitania*. Americans were on this ship and died. The United States declared war in 1917.

Practice

Quote: "Although Joseph Stalin and the Soviet Communists are responsible for the killing of over 20 million of their own people, Hitler and the Nazis are better known for their murderous ways."

Paraphrase: _____
_____
_____
_____

Quote: "The French military officer Napoleon Bonaparte knew how to handle a riotous mob. To quell a protest, he ordered his soldiers to fire cannon directly into civilians. Instead of firing a cannonball, however, Bonaparte ordered his soldiers to pack scrap metal, nails, and bullets into the cannon. This way, more protesters would be killed or wounded."

Paraphrase: _____
_____
_____
_____
_____

7. Thesis Statement

The **thesis statement** is the main idea or argument of your entire essay. It is your main judgment regarding the essay question, and it should contain words used in the prompt. A thesis statement is not a fact. Instead, it is your judgment of the facts. Because of this, a thesis has to be something with which not everyone will agree. Every thesis will provide pieces of evidence in order to provide the reader with a general outline of your essay.

Here is an example from the essay questions "What caused the United States to change from a regional power to a world power? What were the key factors that enabled the United States to emerge in the world as one of the most powerful countries on earth?"

Example 1: The United States changed from a regional power to a world power primarily because of its economic development and its imperialistic philosophy.

This thesis answers the question and provides an outline for the rest of the essay. In the essay, the writer will expand on "economic development" and "imperialistic philosophy."

Come up with two more examples of a thesis based on this question.

| **Example 2:** _____ |
| **Example 3:** _____ |

The Good Thesis Test
If you can answer, "Yes," to these questions, you most likely have a good thesis.

1. Does the thesis address the prompt directly?
2. Does the thesis take a position that I can argue with evidence?
3. Could somebody argue against my thesis statement?

8. Conclusion

The **conclusion** ties the evidence presented in the essay back to the thesis statement. It is the writer's last chance to present how the evidence supports the thesis statement. In a one-paragraph essay, the conclusion can be one sentence, but it may be more.

Here is an example answering the questions "What caused the United States to change from a regional power to a world power? What were the key factors that enabled the United States to emerge in the world as one of the most powerful countries on earth?"

The last two sentences in the following paragraph are the conclusion.

The United States changed from a regional power to a world power primarily because of its economic development and its imperialistic philosophy. Ambitious industrial leaders such as Carnegie and Rockefeller led the urbanization of the late nineteenth century. These men brutally conquered their competition and in the process they urbanized the United States. America quickly became the strongest country in the world. Also, Americans became more imperialistic in their thinking. From the mid–nineteenth century, with the Mexican-American War as the beginning, the United States conquered and took giant areas of land. These areas of land include the American Southwest and islands in the Pacific and in the Caribbean. The United States won in war, or annexed, double its size from 1846 through 1900. **In conclusion, the United States changed from a regional power to a world power because of its economic development and its imperialistic philosophy. It used its power to conquer the American Southwest and islands in the Pacific and Caribbean.**

The Good Conclusion Test
If you can answer, "Yes," to these questions, you have written a good conclusion.

1. Does the conclusion restate the thesis?
2. Does the conclusion include the pieces of evidence from my essay?
3. Does the conclusion help convince the reader that the thesis is correct?

9. Outline for a One-Paragraph Essay

An **outline** helps you organize your thoughts and make sure you have enough evidence to support your thesis statement. An outline does not need to be written in complete sentences, except for the thesis statement and the conclusion. In one paragraph, the more evidence you include, the stronger your argument will be.

An example outline follows to the essay question "What caused the Cold War?"

I. Thesis Statement: "Soviet fears of a third world war and democratic nations' fears of communism caused the Cold War."

Supporting Evidence:

1. Warsaw destruction with no Russian help
2. Potsdam Conference
3. No free elections in Eastern Europe
4. Hungary, 1956
5. Czechoslovakia, 1968
6. German invasion of Russia in WWI and WWII
7. Western hatred of communism

II. Conclusion: Both the Soviets and the free world feared each other greatly. These fears caused the Cold War.

Following this page are two forms, a "Basic Outline Form for a One-Paragraph Essay," and an "Advanced Outline Form for a Paragraph." These forms will help you outline your essay.

Basic Outline Form for a One-Paragraph Essay
(Use complete sentences for the thesis statement and the conclusion.)

I. **Thesis Statement**: _____
_____
    A. Supporting Evidence_____
    B. Supporting Evidence_____
    C. Supporting Evidence_____
II. **Conclusion**: _____
_____

Advanced Outline Form for a One-Paragraph Essay
(Use complete sentences for the thesis statement and the conclusion.)

I. **Thesis Statement**: _____
_____
    A. Supporting Evidence_____
    B. Supporting Evidence_____
    C. Supporting Evidence _____
    D. Supporting Evidence _____
    E. Supporting Evidence_____
II. **Conclusion**: _____
_____

10. Rough Draft of a One-Paragraph Essay

The **rough draft** is the first time that you will explain all the supporting evidence that you use. To do this, take your outline and explain how your evidence supports the thesis statement. Instead of listing your evidence, you will explain its importance.

Here is an example of a rough draft of a one-paragraph essay based on the question "What caused the United States to change from a regional power to a world power? What were the key factors that enabled the United States to emerge in the world as one of the most powerful countries on earth?" The sentences in bold are those that explain how your evidence supports the thesis.

The United States changed from a regional power to a world power primarily because of its economic development and its imperialistic philosophy. Ambitious industrial leaders such as Carnegie and Rockefeller led the urbanization of the late nineteenth century. **These men destroyed their competition, but in the process they urbanized the United States. America quickly became the strongest country in the world.** Also, Americans became more imperialistic in their thinking. From the mid-nineteenth century, with the Mexican-American War as the beginning, the United States conquered and took giant areas of land. These areas of land include the American Southwest and islands in the Pacific and in the Caribbean. The United States won in war, or annexed, double its size from 1846 through 1900. **This land increased changed America. The United States was now a large country and needed a strong military.** In conclusion, the United States changed from a regional power to a world power because of its economic development and its imperialistic philosophy. In the process, it conquered and controlled the American Southwest and islands in the Pacific and Caribbean.

On this page and the next are the basic and advanced rough draft forms.

Basic Rough Draft Form for a One-Paragraph Essay
(Use complete sentences.)

I. Thesis Statement: _____

A. Supporting Evidence: First of all, _____

Explanation: (Explain how the evidence supports the topic sentence) _____

B. Supporting Evidence: Secondly, _____
Explanation: (Explain how the evidence supports the topic sentence) _____

II. **Conclusion**: In conclusion, _____

Advanced Rough Draft Form for a One-Paragraph Essay
(Use complete sentences.)

I. **Thesis Statement**: _____

_____

    A. Supporting Evidence: First of all, _____

Explanation (Explain how this supports the topic sentence): _____

    B. Supporting Evidence: Secondly, _____

Explanation (Explain how this supports the topic sentence): _____

    C. Supporting Evidence: Thirdly, _____

Explanation (Explain how this supports the topic sentence): _____

    D. Supporting Evidence: In addition, _____

Explanation (Explain how this supports the topic sentence): _____

    E. Supporting Evidence: Furthermore, _____

Explanation (Explain how this supports the topic sentence): _____

II. **Conclusion**: _____

_____

Copyright © 2006 by John De Gree. All rights reserved

Chapter III: Skills for the Five-Paragraph Essay

11. Taking Notes

All research papers require the student to read, analyze, and write information that is helpful in answering the question asked. The structure of your note taking depends on the question. Before reading, structure your notes in a way so you will focus on important information and not on unimportant details that would take valuable time. Below is an example of a structure of notes based on the question "What led to the Cold War?" Notice that the last question helps you stick to your topic.

Joseph McCarthy
What?
Who?
When?
Where?
Why?
What role did this term or person play in the Cold War?
Source and page(s):

When taking notes be sure to list the source. You can do this quickly by writing only the last name of the author and the page on which you found the information. This will save you much time later when you are documenting the source in your essay. When you are writing your final essay you don't want to be stuck in the position of rummaging through your papers or flipping through your book, trying to find exactly from where you took your information.

12. Thesis Statement for a Five-Paragraph Essay

The **thesis statement** is the main idea or argument of your entire essay. It is your judgment regarding the essay question and it should contain words used in the prompt. A thesis statement is not a fact. Instead, it is your judgment of the evidence. Because of this, a thesis has to be something with which not everyone will agree. In a five-paragraph essay you should list three pieces of evidence in your thesis in order to provide the reader with an outline of your essay.

Here is an example from the essay question "How did the Cold War affect American society, 1945–1969?" Because this essay requires a five-paragraph response, the student will need three supporting pieces of evidence for the main body. These three should be included in the thesis.

Example 1: The Cold War affected American society from 1945 to 1969 in foreign policy, domestic affairs, and presidential elections.

This thesis answers the question and provides an outline for paragraphs two, three, and four. Paragraph two will detail information about foreign policy, paragraph three about domestic affairs, and paragraph four about presidential elections.

Create two more thesis statements for a five-paragraph essay based on this question.

| **Example 2:** _____ |
| **Example 3:** _____ |

The Good Thesis Test
If you can answer, "Yes," to these questions, you most likely have a good thesis for a five-paragraph essay:

1. Does my thesis address the prompt directly?
2. Does my thesis take a position that I can argue with evidence?
3. Could somebody argue against my thesis statement?

13. The Topic Sentence and the Closer

The **topic sentence** is the main idea of a paragraph in the body of a multiple-paragraph essay. In a five-paragraph essay, a topic sentence takes one of the pieces of evidence in the thesis and states it strongly. The body of this paragraph will support the topic sentence.

Here is one example of a topic sentence for the question "How did the Cold War affect American society, 1945–1969?"
Thesis Statement: The Cold War affected American society from 1945 to 1969 in foreign policy, domestic affairs, and presidential elections.
Topic Sentence for Paragraph Two: The Cold War affected American society from 1945 to 1969 in foreign policy.

Write topic sentences for paragraphs three and four in the box below.

Paragraph Three: _____

Paragraph Four: _____

The Closer

The **closer** ties the evidence presented in the paragraph back to the topic sentence. It is the writer's last chance to present how the evidence supports the topic sentence before moving on. Here is an example regarding the same essay question as above.

The Cold War affected American society from 1945 to 1969 in foreign policy. After the Allied forces destroyed Europe in World War II, the communist and the free nations greatly distrusted each other. Because of this distrust, the United States (U.S.) kept over 300,000 soldiers in Western Europe. Even today, there are approximately 80,000 American soldiers stationed in Germany. The U.S. adopted a policy of containment regarding the communist world to keep communism within its borders and not allow it to expand. Backing up this policy with muscle, the U.S. threatened force in Turkey and Greece when the communist U.S.S.R. threatened civil war. In addition, vast amounts of money were spent rebuilding Europe with the Marshall Plan, and rebuilding defeated Japan, so that these countries could be democratic bulwarks against communism. In Asia, the U.S. fought wars with communist regimes in Korea and in Vietnam. **Based on U.S. actions in Europe and Asia, not to mention Africa, the Middle East, and Latin America, the Cold War dominated American foreign policy from 1945 to 1969.**

14. Outlining a Five-Paragraph Essay

An **outline** is a skeleton for your essay. Here, you organize your essay before writing it out in complete sentences. If you have a framework first, it will be fairly easy to write the essay. Below is an explanation of writing an outline for a five-paragraph essay.

A. First Paragraph
   For the first paragraph, it is enough to write down the thesis and list the three topics that will be your body paragraphs.

B. Body Paragraphs
   1. Organize your paragraphs into topics by following the order you wrote in the thesis. Your thesis should have listed three topics. The first will be the topic of your second paragraph, the second the topic of your third paragraph, and the third the topic of your fourth paragraph.
   2. You do not need to write complete sentences for your outline. It is enough to write the topics of each paragraph and to list the supporting evidence for your topic sentence in your outline. You will add more information when you write your draft.
   3. Document each source! Write the author's last name and the page where you found this information.

C. Conclusion:
   The conclusion is the place where you restate your thesis and your topic sentences. You will convince the reader better by a reminder at the end what your essay was all about. After the restatements, finish the essay with strong words supporting your thesis.

Following this page are two forms — one basic and one advanced — to help you develop your outline.

Basic Outline Form for a Five-Paragraph Essay

(Use complete sentences for the thesis, topic sentences, closers, and conclusion.)

Paragraph I.
Thesis Statement: _____
_____

Paragraph II.
I. Topic Sentence: _____
_____

      A. Supporting Evidence:_____
      B. Supporting Evidence:_____
II. Closer: _____
_____Write the source:_____

Paragraph III.
I. Topic Sentence: _____
_____

      A. Supporting Evidence:_____
      B. Supporting Evidence:_____
II. Closer: _____
_____Write the source:_____

Paragraph IV.
I. Topic Sentence: _____
_____

      A. Supporting Evidence:_____
      B. Supporting Evidence:_____
II. Closer: _____
_____Write the source:_____

Paragraph V. Conclusion
I. Restate thesis statement: _____
_____

II. Strong statement that shows how the topic sentences support the thesis:_____
_____

Advanced Outline Form for a Five-Paragraph Essay

(Use complete sentences for the thesis, topic sentences, closers, and conclusion.)

Paragraph I.
Thesis Statement: _____
_____

Paragraph II.
I. Topic Sentence: _____
_____

      A. Supporting Evidence:_____
      B. Supporting Evidence: _____
      C. Supporting Evidence:_____
      D. Supporting Evidence:_____
      E. Supporting Evidence:_____
II. Closer: _____
_____Write the source:_____

Paragraph III.
I. Topic Sentence: _____
_____

      A. Supporting Evidence:_____
      B. Supporting Evidence: _____
      C. Supporting Evidence:_____
      D. Supporting Evidence:_____
      E. Supporting Evidence:_____
II. Closer: _____
_____Write the source:_____

Paragraph IV. Use another page or the back of this paper.
Paragraph V. Conclusion
I. Restate thesis statement: _____
_____
_____

II. Strong Statement that shows how the topic sentences support the thesis:_____
_____
_____

15. Writing a Rough Draft for a Five-Paragraph Essay

A.   **Introductory Paragraph**
The Social Studies essay begins directly with the thesis, unless the paper is meant to be longer than five-paragraphs. Following the thesis is a brief explanation of the main topics that will be written in detail in the body paragraphs. Below is an example response to the essay question "How did the Cold War affect American society from 1945 to 1969?" (The Thesis Statement is in bold).

The Cold War affected American society from 1945 to 1969 in foreign policy, domestic affairs, and presidential elections. In foreign policy, the United States acted on a broad front to combat the spread of communism. In Latin America, in Asia, in the Middle East, and in Europe, American dollars and soldiers were utilized in peacetime activities and in war to prevent the spread of communism. Domestically, issues of the Cold War dominated life and politics. Americans built bomb shelters and students practiced war emergencies. Politicians hounded Americans believed to be communist sympathizers. In presidential elections, the key theme in foreign policy was, "How will you confront, or communicate, with the U.S.S.R.?" Americans were concerned with how a president would represent his country with the communist world.

B.   **The Body**
The body of your essay is where you present your evidence to prove your thesis. In these paragraphs, you will present your evidence and explain how it supports the topic sentence. An example of this is found in Skill #10, Rough Draft of a One-Paragraph Essay. Keep the order of your arguments the same as the order of mention in the thesis. Attempt to order the events chronologically.

C.   **Conclusion**
In this paragraph, you need to restate your thesis, tie the topic sentences of your body paragraphs to the thesis, and leave the reader with the strongest evidence that supports your argument. Your job is to convince the reader that your position is correct. Write strongly.

Following this page are two forms — one basic and one advanced — to help you develop your rough draft.

Basic Rough Draft Form for a Five-Paragraph Essay
(Use complete sentences. Use the back when you need space.)

Paragraph I.
Thesis Statement: _____
_____

Paragraph II.
Topic Sentence: _____
_____

A. Supporting Evidence: First of all, _____
_____

Explanation (Explain how the evidence supports the thesis): _____
_____

B. Supporting Evidence: Secondly, _____
_____

Explanation (Explain how the evidence supports the thesis): _____
_____

II. Closer: In conclusion, _____
_____

Paragraphs III and IV. Follow the structure of paragraph II.

Paragraph V. Conclusion
I. Restate thesis statement: _____
_____

II. Strong statement that shows how the topic sentences support the thesis: _____
_____

Copyright © 2006 by John De Gree. All rights reserved

Advanced Rough Draft Form for a Five-Paragraph Essay
(Use complete sentences.)

Paragraph I.
I. Thesis Statement: _____
_____

Paragraph II.
I. Topic Sentence: _____
_____

A. Supporting Evidence: First of all, _____
_____

Explanation (Explain how this supports the thesis): _____
_____

B. Supporting Evidence: Secondly, _____
_____

Explanation (Explain how this supports the thesis): _____
_____

C. Supporting Evidence: Thirdly, _____
_____

Explanation (Explain how this supports the thesis): _____
_____

D. Supporting Evidence: In addition, _____
_____

Explanation (Explain how this supports the thesis): _____
_____

E. Supporting Evidence: Furthermore, _____
_____

Explanation (Explain how this supports the thesis): _____
_____

II. Closer: _____
_____

Paragraphs III and IV. Follow the same structure as above.

Paragraph V. Conclusion
I. Restate thesis statement: _____
_____

II. Strong statement that shows how the topic sentences support the thesis:
_____
_____

16. Revising

After writing the rough draft, it is necessary to revise. Revising involves four steps. Take your essay and perform these four tasks with a red pen in hand.

STEP I   Deletion

Delete dead words: the end, every, just, nice, great, bad, got, everything, getting, so, well, a lot, lots, get, good, some, yours, you, your very

STEP II   Addition

A. Add words, facts, or better descriptions. Imagine you are writing for an adult who does not know the subject well. Explain every point precisely.
B. Use transitions whenever helpful.

To add ideas
further, furthermore, moreover, in addition

To show results
therefore, consequently, as a result

To indicate order
first, second, in addition to

To summarize
to sum up, to summarize, in short

To compare
similarly, likewise, by comparison

Conclusion
In conclusion, to conclude, finally

STEP III   Substitution

Substitute repetitive words and weak-sounding words.
A. Underline the first word in each sentence. If the words are the same, change some of the words.
B. Read your thesis, topic sentences, closers, and conclusion; change words as needed. Is your word choice powerful and effective? Will your essay convince the reader?

STEP IV   Rearrangement

Write sentences that have a variety of beginnings.

Adjective beginnings
Well-equipped, dedicated Union soldiers won the American Civil War.

"ing" words
Riding horses was common among most 1800s Americans.

Prepositional Phrases
Over the vast Pacific Ocean, Columbus sailed.

Dependent Clauses
Because of Lincoln, the North did not give up the war effort.

"ly" words
Bravely, Washington led the Continental Army to victory.

Adverbs
Slowly, but surely, Grant moved the Union Army

17. Documenting Sources in the Text

When you take information from a source and use it in a paragraph, you cite it at the end of the paragraph. Place in parentheses the author's name and the page number you found the information. For example, if you've found out information on the Cold War in America from a textbook written by Robert De Gree, you would cite it as the last sentence in the example below.

The Cold War affected American society from 1945 to 1969 in foreign policy. After the Allied forces destroyed Europe in World War II, the communist and the free nations greatly distrusted each other. Because of this distrust, the United States (U.S.) kept over 300,000 U.S. soldiers in Western Europe. Even today, there are approximately 80,000 U.S. soldiers stationed in Germany alone. The U.S. adopted a policy of containment regarding the communist world. The U.S. would keep communism within its borders, and not allow it to expand. Backing up this policy with muscle, the U.S. threatened force in Turkey and Greece when communist U.S.S.R. threatened civil war. In addition, vast amounts of money were spent rebuilding Europe with the Marshall Plan, and rebuilding defeated Japan, so that these countries could be democratic bulwarks against communism. In Asia, the U.S. fought wars with communist regimes in Korea and in Vietnam. Based on U.S. actions in Europe and Asia, not to mention Africa, the Middle East, and Latin America, the Cold War dominated American foreign policy from 1945 to 1969 (De Gree, pages 399-450).

Note: This is according to Gibaldi, Joseph, <u>MLA Handbook for Writers of Research Papers,</u> (New York: The Modern Language Association of America, 1995).

18. Works Cited

At the end of your document, on a separate piece of paper, write "Works Cited" at the top middle. After this, write your sources in alphabetical order using the following format:

Book
Author (Last Name, First Name). <u>Title of Book</u>. Place of publication: Publisher, date. (If there is more than one author, list them in alphabetical order with a comma in between names.)

Author of one chapter in a book
Author (Last Name, First Name). "Title of chapter." <u>Title of Book</u>. Place of Publication: Publisher, date. Pages of chapter.

Dictionary
<u>Title of Dictionary</u>. Edition.

Internet
Author (if known). "Document Title." <u>Website or Database Title</u>. Date of electronic publication (if known). Name of sponsoring institution (if known). Date information was accessed <URL>.

Encyclopedia
"Article." <u>Encyclopedia Title</u>. Edition.

Interview or Lecture
Name of Speaker (Last Name, First Name). "Title of interview or lecture." Place of interview or lecture, date.

Note: This is according to Gibaldi, Joseph, <u>MLA Handbook for Writers of Research Papers</u>, (New York: The Modern Language Association of America, 1995).

19. Typing Guidelines

1. All final research papers must be typed. The Works Cited page must also be typed.
2. The font must be a standard typeface and style. Courier, Helvetica, and Times are good choices. Do not use italics, handwriting, or anything else decorative.
3. The size of the letters must be 12 points.
4. All margins must be one inch from the top, bottom, and each side.
5. All sentences will be double-spaced.
6. Pages will be numbered in the lower right-hand side of the page. Do not number your Cover page. The Works Cited page is numbered but does not count as a text page.

20. The Cover Page and Checklist

Cover Page

The Cover page needs to have the title of your research paper centered. It can be at the top, the middle, or the bottom of the page. You need to make an illustration by drawing in pencil, coloring in colored pencils, or using any other teacher-approved medium.

In the bottom right-hand corner, write or type your name, date, and period of your social studies teacher.

Checklist

All final papers must have these items turned in to your social studies teacher on the final due date.

Inside of a clear, plastic folder include the following items in this order:

1. Cover page   _____
2. Final draft   _____
3. Works Cited page   _____
4. Prewriting   _____
5. Outline   _____
6. Rough draft   _____

Chapter IV: Skills for the Multi-Page Essay

21. Thesis Statement for a Multi-Page Essay

As explained earlier in this book, the thesis statement is the main idea or argument of your entire essay. It is your judgment regarding the essay question and may contain the same words from the prompt. A thesis statement is not a fact. Instead, it is your judgment of the evidence. Because of this, a thesis has to be something with which not everyone will agree. In a multi-page essay, the writer need not list all the evidence he will present to support the thesis statement. However, general topics of evidence need to be presented so that the reader is aware of what the essay will entail.

A multi-page research paper represents a great deal of effort and will not be written during a timed test. Therefore, the writer may choose to write an introduction to the essay, or what some writers call a hook. Before you write the thesis, include a short, interesting introduction.

Here is an example from the essay question "How did the Cold War affect American society?"

Example 1: Humphrey wiped the sweat from his brow. He looked nervously around the room, searching for a friendly face. Nobody in the room was willing to give him the slightest nod of approval throughout the questioning. He feared not only for his job but also for his family and life altogether. Humphrey was a Hollywood actor. The time was 1954. Senator Joseph McCarthy was busy finding actors and actresses who had any ties to the Communists. In 1954, an actor who had ties with the Communists would never work again. He was "blacklisted." The Cold War affected American society by pitting some Americans against each other.

The Good Thesis Test
If you can answer, "Yes," to these questions, you most likely have a good thesis for a multi-page essay:

1. Does the thesis directly address the prompt?
2. Does my thesis take a position that I can argue with evidence?
3. Could somebody argue against my thesis statement?

22. Counterargument

In social studies, many historians have different judgments based on the same evidence. For example, some historians view the Korean War as a success, and others view it as a great loss. These are two very different judgments on U.S. history. These two judgments can be called two **perspectives**.

When you defend your thesis statement, you should include at least one counterargument. A **counterargument** is one in which the writer presents an idea that goes against his thesis statement. Then, in that paragraph, the writer shows how this idea is wrong.

For example, imagine if the thesis statement to an essay were, "The Korean War was a monumental failure in U.S. foreign policy." The counterargument paragraph for this thesis should be at the end of the essay, perhaps right before the conclusion paragraph.

Here is an example of a counterargument paragraph:

Some historians may claim that the Korean War was a great success of U.S. foreign policy. They claim that the protection of free Korea kept the Communists in check around the world, and that Americans served a great purpose in dying for other people. Containment, the U.S. policy of keeping world communism to its borders and fighting its expanse, was a false response to communism. World communism was not united, but divided. The Communists in Asia were not united with the Communists in Europe. In fact, the U.S.S.R. and China had troops facing each other at their respective borders because of their distrust. The Warsaw Pact in Europe was a union of European Communist countries to cooperate militarily. Communist China and Communist Korea were not part of this pact. The Communists in Asia were not united with the Communists of Europe, and the conflict in Korea was primarily a regional one, not a global one. U.S. intervention in Korea cost Americans over 50,000 lives, and it was in the end, a precursor to the mistakes of the Vietnam War.

Notice that the beginning of the paragraph above begins with the words "Some historians say." This is because you are presenting an idea that is opposite of yours. In your paragraph, be clear that you think these people are wrong.

23. Analyzing Primary Sources

When you read history and try to analyze it, pay attention to details of the document that tell you important details of the source. These small details can give you incredible insight as to how you should analyze the historical information. Here are a few basic questions to which you should find answers, while you are analyzing historical texts, paintings, or any historical documents.

1. Who wrote (drew, illustrated) it? What position does the writer have? Is the writer a professor, an author of novels? Is the author(s) respected in the field? Did multiple authors prepare the text?

2. Who is (was) the audience? Students? Bookstore customers? Newspaper readers? Magazine readers?

3. When was the text written (drawn/ illustrated)? Was it written during a critical time of history that the text is about? Was it written many years after the time of history it is written about? Are historians more biased about events that happen during our lifetime?

4. Who paid for the text to be written? Is there a chance that the author(s) will be biased because of who is paying for the text?

5. Where was the text written? Was the text written in a place that is in the middle of the historical study the text is about? Is it possible the author can be biased based on where it was written? What country is the author from? Is it possible the country might affect someone's perspective?

6. Who is the publisher? Could the publisher have a bias that might affect the veracity (truth) of the materials?

7. Why was the text written? What was the purpose of the text? Was it meant to be part of a textbook? Was it meant to stir emotions for or against the government?

24. Cause and Effect

Cause and effect is a term that means one event made another event happen. For example, if you push against the pedals of your bicycle, the bicycle moves. In this example, the push against the pedals is the cause and the bicycle moving is the effect.

CAUSE ------------------------------→EFFECT
push against pedals--------------→bicycle moves

In social studies, cause and effect usually relates events and people. The relationship is trickier to understand than the above example with the bicycle. Sometimes it is difficult to see causes and effects in history. Here are two examples from American history with which most historians would agree.

CAUSE -----------------------------------→EFFECT
Japan attacks Pearl Harbor--------→the United States enters World War II
the U.S. drops atomic bombs on Japan -------→Japan surrenders

Now, write five causes and effects from history.

Term (Cause)	Effect
1. The North won the Civil War.	1. The U.S. did not break up in 1865.
2._____	2._____
3._____	3._____
4._____	4._____
5._____	5._____

25. Compare and Contrast

To **compare** means to look at two or more objects and recognize what they have in common. To **contrast** means to look at two or more objects and recognize what they have different from each other.

Try to compare and contrast President Reagan with President Carter.

Ronald Reagan		**Jimmy Carter**
Differences	**Similarities**	**Differences**
Republican	Both politicians	Democrat

26. Outline and Rough Draft for a Multi-Page Essay

In a longer essay, the only item that differs structurally from the smaller essays is the introductory paragraph. In smaller essays that are from one to two pages the introduction should begin with the thesis statement. In longer essays, the writer can begin with information that will catch the reader's attention and add the thesis at the end of the paragraph. Read the sample introductory paragraph below for the essay question "Was the Civil War necessary?" Notice that the last sentence is the thesis statement.

The American Civil War is the bloodiest war in our country's history. More than 500,000 Americans died. Brother fought against brother. Townspeople took up arms against each other. Great suffering became commonplace. Even so, because of the Civil War our nation has never faced another challenge to its unity. In over 140 years not one state has ever tried to secede or rebel from the United States. More importantly, the Civil War ended slavery on American soil. Millions of slaves were forever released from bondage into freedom. Without the Civil War, nobody knows for how long slavery would have continued. Even though the American Civil War was a tragic war; it was good and necessary.

For further help on outlining and writing a rough draft for a multi-page essay: See the following pages for outline and rough draft forms.

Basic Outline Form for a Multi-Page Essay
(Use complete sentences for thesis, topic sentences, closers, and conclusion.)

Paragraph I.
Thesis Statement: _____
_____

Paragraph II.
I. Topic Sentence: _____
_____
      A. Supporting Evidence:_____
      B. Supporting Evidence:_____
II. Closer: _____
_____Write the source:_____

Remaining Body Paragraphs.
Follow the same structure as paragraph II.

Paragraph V. Conclusion
I. Restate thesis statement: _____
_____
_____

II. Strong statement that shows how the topic sentences support the thesis:
_____
_____

Advanced Outline Form for a Multi-Page Essay

(Use complete sentences for thesis, topic sentences, closers, and conclusion.)

Paragraph I.
Thesis Statement: _____
_____

Paragraph II.
I. Topic Sentence: _____
_____
      A. Supporting Evidence: _____
      B. Supporting Evidence: _____
      C. Supporting Evidence: _____
      D. Supporting Evidence: _____
      E. Supporting Evidence: _____
II. Closer: _____
_____Write the source: _____

Remaining Body Paragraphs.
Follow the same structure as paragraph II.

Paragraph V. Conclusion
I. Restate thesis statement: _____
_____
_____

II. Strong statement that shows how the topic sentences support the thesis: _____
_____

Basic Rough Draft Form for a Multi-Page Essay
(Use complete sentences. Use the back when you need space.)

Paragraph I.
Thesis Statement: _____
_____

Paragraph II.
I. Topic Sentence: _____
_____

    A. Supporting Evidence: First of all, _____
_____

Explanation (Explain how this supports the topic sentence):_____
_____

    B. Supporting Evidence: Secondly, _____
_____

Explanation (Explain how this supports the topic sentence): _____
_____

II. Closer: Show how A and B support the topic sentence. In conclusion, _____
_____

Write the source: _____

Remaining Body Paragraphs.
Follow the same structure as paragraph II.

Paragraph V. Conclusion
I. Restate thesis statement: _____
_____

II. Strong statement that shows how the topic sentences support the thesis: _____
_____
_____

Advanced Rough Draft Form for a Multi-Page Essay
(Use complete sentences. Use the back when you need space.)

Paragraph I.
Thesis Statement: _____

_____

Paragraph II.
I. Topic Sentence: _____

    A. Supporting Evidence: _____

Explanation (Explain how this supports the topic sentence): _____

    B. Supporting Evidence: _____

Explanation (Explain how this supports the topic sentence): _____

    C. Supporting Evidence: _____

Explanation (Explain how this supports the topic sentence): _____

    D. Supporting Evidence: _____

Explanation (Explain how this supports the topic sentence): _____

    E. Supporting Evidence: _____

Explanation (Explain how this supports the topic sentence): _____

II. Closer: Show how A and B support the topic sentence: _____

Write the source: _____

Remaining Body Paragraphs.
Follow the same structure as paragraph II.

Paragraph V. Conclusion
I. Restate thesis statement: _____

_____

II. Strong statement that shows how the topic sentences support the thesis: _____

_____

Chapter V: Grading Rubrics

One-Paragraph Essay Grading Rubric

Grading Scale
4   Exceeds Standards
3   Meets Standards
2   Approaching Standards
1   Below Standards
0   Nonexistent

                                                                        Y/N

I.   Thesis Statement:
      Does it persuasively answer the question?
                                      Score _____

II.   Evidence Used:
      Are two or more relevant pieces of evidence used?
                                        Score _____

III. Evidence Explained
      Is the evidence explained correctly and persuasively?
                                        Score _____

IV.   Conclusion:
      Does the evidence strengthen the topic sentence?
                                        Score _____

V.   Prewriting Activities
      Are all prewriting activities included and attached
      to the final?
                                        Score _____

                    Total Addition of Scores = _____
                                                   X 5
                                    Score = _____

Spelling or Grammatical Errors   -_____
Missing Prewriting Work   -_____

                                  Final Score = _____

Five-Paragraph Essay Grading Rubric

Grading Scale
4   Exceeds Standards
3   Meets Standards
2   Approaching Standards
1   Below Standards
0   Nonexistent

Paragraph I.   Yes/No
A. Thesis: Does it answer the question and provide organizational structure? _____
B. Interest?   Does it grab the interest of the reader? _____
                               Score: _____

Paragraph II.
A. Topic Sentence: Does it provide a strong statement supporting the thesis? _____
B. Evidence: 1. Is evidence used to support the topic sentence? _____
                     2. Is the evidence explained clearly and in detail? _____
C. Closer: Does the closer convincingly link the paragraph's evidence
                     with the topic sentence? _____
                               Score: _____

Paragraph III.
A. Topic Sentence: Does it provide a strong statement supporting the thesis? _____
B. Evidence: 1. Is evidence used to support the topic sentence? _____
                     2. Is the evidence explained clearly and in detail? _____
C. Closer: Does the closer convincingly link the paragraph's evidence
                     with the topic sentence? _____
                               Score: _____

Paragraph IV.
A. Topic Sentence: Does it provide a strong statement supporting the thesis? _____
B. Evidence: 1. Is evidence used to support the topic sentence? _____
                     2. Is the evidence explained clearly and in detail? _____
C. Closer: Does the closer convincingly link the evidence
                     with the topic sentence? _____
                               Score: _____

Paragraph V.
A. Restating Topic Sentences: Are the topic sentences in II, III, IV restated? _____
B. Closer: Does the Closer persuasively show that the main ideas of
     paragraphs II, III, and IV strongly support the thesis? _____

                               Score: _____ X 5 = _____
           Spelling or Grammatical Errors   -_____
           Missing Prewriting Work   -_____

           Total Score   _____

Social Studies - Multi-Page Research Essay Grading Rubric

Grading Scale
4   Exceeds Standards
3   Meets Standards
2   Approaching Standards
1   Below Standards
0   Nonexistent

I.   Organization/Structure of the Essay   Y/N
A. Thesis: Does the thesis take a firm position on the essay topic?   _____
B. Topic Sentences: Do topic sentences strongly support the thesis?   _____
C. Conclusion: Does the conclusion persuasively affirm the thesis?   _____
    Score: _____

II   Evidence: Part I: Accuracy and Adequacy of Evidence
A. Accuracy: Is all evidence accurate (true)?   _____
B. Adequacy: Is enough evidence used?   _____
    Score: _____

III   Evidence: Part II: Validity and Persuasiveness of Evidence
B. Validity: Do explanations of evidence make sense?   _____
A. Persuasiveness: Do explanations of evidence support main ideas?   _____
    Score: _____

IV   Language Mechanics
A. Punctuation: Does the essay use correct punctuation?   _____
B. Grammar: Does the essay use correct grammar (sentence structure)?   _____
C. Spelling: Is spelling correct?   _____
    Score: _____

V   Writing Process
A. Prewriting Activities: Are all prewriting activities complete?   _____
B. Effort: Is great effort shown in these activities?   _____
    Score: _____

Total Score: _____ X 5 = Grade: _____

Copyright © 2006 by John De Gree. All rights reserved

Made in the USA
San Bernardino, CA
01 February 2019